The Church of Holy Apostles
5211 W. Bull Valley Road
McHenry, IL 60050
815-385-LORD (5673)

The Church of Holy Apostles

W9-BDF-691

The Church of Holy Apostles
5211 W. Bull Valley Road
McHenry, IL 60050
815-385-LORD (5673)

Come Wor

A Journey

ship
With Me

through the Church Year

Written by
RUTH L. BOLING

Illustrated by
TRACEY DAHLE CARRIER

G Geneva Press
GENEVA Louisville, Kentucky

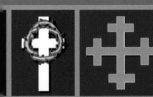

Text © 2001 Ruth L. Boling
Illustrations and book design © 2001 Tracey Dahle Carrier

First edition
Published by Geneva Press
Louisville, Kentucky

PRINTED IN HONG KONG

01 02 03 04 05 06 07 08 09 10 — 10 9 8 7 6 5 4 3 2

Library of Congress Cataloging-in-Publication Data

Boling, Ruth L.
    Come worship with me : a journey through the church year / by Ruth L. Boling ;
illustrated by Tracey Dahle Carrier.
        p.   cm.
    ISBN 0-664-50045-5
    1. Church year—Juvenile literature. [1. Church year. 2. Christianity. 3. God.] I. Carrier,
Tracey Dahle, ill. II. Title
BV30.B63 2000
263'.9—dc21   00-039313

For Daniel,
Child of mine, child of God.

~RB

For Charlie and Chas,
Whose contribution through support and
enthusiasm has been immeasurable.

With love,
~TDC

Message from the Author

The church year begins four Sundays before Christmas with the preparatory season of Advent. Its high point comes during Holy Week and Easter with the commemoration of Jesus' death and resurrection. A well-worn familiarity with the rhythms and themes of the church year can widen our understanding of who God is, how God cares for us, and what God asks of us in our daily lives.

Each season or special holiday of the church emerges from a set of biblical stories, and each focuses our attention on particular truths about God drawn from those stories. As the church year unfolds, truth is layered upon truth. Colors, actions, symbols, words, and song combine to evoke the great mysteries of the faith, making them accessible to children of every age.

Ruth L. Boling

Table of Contents

Come With Me 9

Come To My Church 11

Advent 13

Christmas 15

Epiphany 19

Ordinary Time 21

Ash Wednesday 23

Lent 25

Palm Sunday 27

Maundy Thursday 29

Good Friday 31

Easter 33

Pentecost 37

Trinity 39

All Saints' Day 41

Advent 43

Christian Symbols and Crosses 44

 # Come With Me

Come with me to a special place, a place where God is.

I know God is everywhere, rustling in the long meadow grass, whispering on the winds high above, singing chick-a-dee-dee-dee with the birds in the trees.

I know God is with me all the time, when I'm walking outdoors in the rain, when I'm tucked snug in my bed at night, or when I'm first to wake up in the morning and the whole house is quiet.

I know God is everywhere, but in one special place I feel closer to God than I do anywhere else.

 Come with me.

Come To My Church

We worship God here, and that's when I feel God the most.

I feel God when the music begins and the rumbling organ pipes make my feet tingle right through the floor. I feel God when our pastor smiles at us and says, "Good morning!" I feel God when the singing starts, and my dad and I share a hymnbook. He loves to sing.

I feel God when the whole church grows silent just before we pray. Then, even my little sister sits still and stops whispering.

I feel God on ordinary days and on special days, all year long. You can feel God, too.

 Come worship with me.

Advent

It's a new year in our church. Advent. We are waiting for Christmas. We are waiting and waiting and waiting. It's hard to wait. Do you see the candles in the Advent wreath? They help us count the Sundays until Christmas. One, two, three, four. The white candle in the middle is the Christ candle. We wait to light it on Christmas Eve.

During Advent we ask God to come and be with us. We sing "O Come, O Come Emmanuel" and other songs of hope. At night we visit people who are too old to come to church. We sing carols with them. They are waiting, too.

We decorate by hanging the greens. We use evergreens because God is everywhere and everlasting. Everybody helps. The sanctuary smells like a pine forest.

The children trim the tree with ornaments that teach about God. My favorite is the scroll with tiny Hebrew writing on it. The words say, "Prepare Ye the Way of the Lord." I like that, because we're preparing for Jesus' birthday. It is almost here!

The Bible tells us how to prepare, by sharing with others, treating people fairly, and being kind. Are you prepared?

 God is near.

Christmas

Brrrr. . . . We're bundled in our coats when we get to church tonight, but inside feels warm and holy. We can't help whispering to each other because we're so excited. Our parents say, "Shhhh!" but it doesn't work. When the beautiful carol music begins, everyone finally quiets down. It is Christmas Eve.

"In those days a decree went out from Caesar Augustus," the pastor reads, and we listen to the story of baby Jesus, the angels, and the shepherds in the little town of Bethlehem. We open our hymnbooks and sing what the angels sang, "Gloria in Excelsis Deo." We bow our heads and pray for peace on earth.

Finally comes the moment everyone's been waiting for. A family goes forward to the Advent wreath. Someone will light the Christ candle. Who will it be? Watch and see. The light shines in the darkness. The Son of God is born!

The ushers pass the light to everyone in the sanctuary. I hold my candle . . . steady, steady . . . while I light yours. Now you hold your candle . . . steady, steady . . . while you light the next one. Watch how the soft glow spreads. See how people's eyes shine. We sing "Silent Night, Holy Night" and I snuggle with my dad.

I love the quiet. I love the light. I love this night.

 God is with us.

Epiphany

Twelve days after Christmas comes Epiphany. "Behold, wise men came from the East," the Bible says. They followed a star all the way to Bethlehem in search of a newborn king. When they saw Jesus, they knew they were also seeing God.

Some people think the wise men were really kings. No one knows for sure, but we always sing "We Three Kings" on Epiphany. With each slow beat of the music I imagine the wise men swaying on their camels as they ride through the desert. I imagine them drawing their robes tightly around themselves against the cold desert wind. I imagine them opening a stable door, only to find a poor family with a tiny baby sleeping in the straw next to goats, sheep, and clucking chickens.

Could this be the newborn king? The wise men know that it is. They kneel down and worship the baby. Opening their saddlebags, they give him great handfuls of gold, frankincense, and myrrh. Then they mount their camels to ride home and tell others.

On Epiphany, we try to be like the wise men. We give to families who are poor or who have no homes, and we tell others about Jesus. We can give food or money, clothes, or even blankets. We can tell about God's love and about Jesus' birthday. What will you give? Who will you tell?

 Sometimes we can see God.

 # Ordinary Time

In between the special seasons at church there is Ordinary Time. When we worship God during Ordinary Time we celebrate God's everyday blessings. A blessing is something given by God. Food is a blessing. Hope is a blessing. So are snow days, good friends, and whistling. Blessings are everywhere. We can thank God for them by serving God.

Jesus served God. He preached good news to poor people. He healed sick people. He made friends with people that nobody else liked. He showed God's love to all. Jesus was a great leader. He taught us to lead by serving.

There are many ways to serve. Here at church, we can serve as worship leaders.

I am a worship leader when I stand on tiptoe to light the candles at the beginning of the service and snuff them out at the end. Everybody watches. I am a worship leader when I shake people's hands at the front door and say, "Good morning!" or when I pass the offering plates, or sing with the junior choir, or raise my hand to share a joy or concern before the pastor's prayer.

I wonder if I could ever preach a sermon. That would be hard.

 God calls us to serve.

Ash Wednesday

It's not Sunday, it's Wednesday. We come to church today to think about serious things. We think about how we do not always love God or love others the way Jesus did. Then we repent. We tell God we are sorry for our sins and we promise to change our ways. I tell God I am sorry for being greedy, and I promise to share. Are you sorry for something? Tell God and make a promise. God will forgive you.

On Ash Wednesday we think about something that's even more serious. One day when it is time for our lives to be over, we will die. "Ashes to ashes," the Bible says, "dust to dust." Even Jesus died.

We walk to the front of the church while quiet music plays, and we form a line. When we get to the front of the line, our pastor rubs ashes on our foreheads in the shape of a small, gray cross, and then whispers something to us in our ear. The ashes remind us that one day we will die, but the shape of the cross reminds us that whether we live or whether we die, we are not alone.

 We belong to God.

Lent

It's a new season in our church. Lent. We are waiting again, but this time we are waiting for Easter. We have to wait forty days! While we wait we remember the promises we made on Ash Wednesday and we try to change our ways. Do you remember your promise?

Jesus waited in the wilderness once for forty days without eating or drinking anything. He prayed to God the whole time. He was tempted by the devil to give up, but he didn't. We must try very hard not to give up either.

Everyone seems quieter during Lent. Everyone thinks and everyone prays. When I pray I talk softly to God in my mind. Sometimes I talk out loud. Sometimes I thank God for things and sometimes I ask God to be with people who are lonely or afraid. During Lent, I always ask God to help me keep my promises.

Sometimes I write letters to God or draw pictures for God. Even the songs we sing in church are prayers. Did you know that?

Our pastor says praying isn't just for church. We can pray at home, at school, before meals, at bedtime, and even on our way to soccer. The Bible says, "Pray at all times."

 God listens.

Palm Sunday

"Hosanna!" we shout. "Hosanna!" we sing. Everybody gets palms from a real palm tree on their way in to worship this morning. We march down the aisle waving them high in the air. We sing lots of songs today and most of them are loud. The little kids sing too. Everybody loves that.

Long ago on this day Jesus rode into Jerusalem on a donkey. Crowds cheered him. They spread cloaks and palm branches in his path. They followed him into the city and called him "King." They were afraid of the rulers of their land and they wanted Jesus to save them.

I hold my palm during worship and stroke the smooth, flat sides between my fingers while our pastor talks about what will happen to Jesus next. Some kids flick their palms at each other like whips until their parents say, "Stop that!" My mom always folds hers into the shape of a cross.

I'm not sure whether to be glad or sad on Palm Sunday, because I know Jesus will die soon on the cross. I will try to be glad, because he is the "King of Kings." When I feel afraid, I will ask him to save me, too.

 With God we are safe.

Maundy Thursday

Just a few days after the crowds followed Jesus into Jerusalem, he ate his Last Supper with his friends. He gave them bread to eat and wine to drink. "This bread is my body," he told them. "This wine is my blood. Do this to remember me." From that day on, Jesus would be with his friends in a special way each time they shared this meal. Jesus loved his friends.

Tonight our pastors serve us the Lord's Supper. One lifts a loaf of bread high in the air, breaks it in two, and shows us the broken halves. The other pours a long ribbon of grape juice from a special pitcher into a special cup and says, "Our Savior invites all who trust in him to share the feast."

We pass plates of bread to everybody in the church. When the pastor says, "This is the body of Christ," we eat the bread. Everyone is quiet for a minute. Then we pass trays with tiny cups of grape juice to everybody in the church. The trays are very heavy. When our pastor says, "This is the blood of Christ," we drink from our cups.

Jesus is with us in a special way at the Lord's Supper. We are his friends, too.

 Jesus loves us.

 # Good Friday

Jesus loved us so much that he died for us. That's what's good about Good Friday, but when I think about the Son of God dying, I don't feel so good. Do you?

Besides, it's dark outside right now and almost past my bedtime. There is nothing pretty to look at in the church tonight. There are no flowers and no bright colors and even the cross is draped in black. I don't like it.

After the Last Supper, Jesus went with his friends to a garden to pray. He was arrested there. The next day was Friday. Crowds of angry people came to see him and make fun of him. "Crucify him!" they shouted. Jesus was whipped and hung on the cross. He died and was buried.

We listen to this story from the Bible while someone snuffs out the candles one by one. The sanctuary grows darker, darker, dark. A lady with a low voice sings "Were You There When They Crucified My Lord?" I get the shivers.

"It is finished." The story ends. We leave in silence.

 God is sad.

Easter

It's still dark when my mom wakes me. She doesn't even make me comb my hair. Everybody is still yawning when they get to church. We don't go inside. Instead, we all walk uphill together as the sky turns from gray to pinkish blue. Just as the golden sun slips over the edge of the earth, the Sunrise Service begins.

"Christ is risen!" we say. "Christ is risen indeed!" One of the teenagers strums his guitar and we sing glad songs in the morning light. Jesus died on the cross, but now he is alive again. He will live with God forever, and we will too, after we die. This is God's plan.

We hurry home to eat breakfast and change clothes, because we're going back! My mom says to wear my good tie since everyone dresses up on Easter. The church is almost full when we get there. We can smell the Easter flowers even before we go inside. There are red tulips, yellow daffodils, and Easter lilies that look like small white trumpets. There are real trumpets, too.

Our pastor stands and reads the story of the women who came to Jesus' tomb and found the stone rolled away. The tomb was empty. Jesus appeared to the women and said, "Greetings!" He also said, "Do not be afraid."

"Tah-tah-tah-taaaaah!" the trumpets sound. We stand and sing "Jesus Christ Is Risen Today." My dad closes his eyes while he sings. He knows all the words.

I love Easter even more than Christmas. It's the most important day of the year.

 God is alive.

Pentecost

Today is the Church's birthday. On this day long ago the Church was born. It happened like this:

Jesus' friends were together in one room feeling frightened and sad because Jesus had left them to go back to God. Suddenly they heard the rushing sound of a mighty wind, and they saw flickerings of red, like flames of fire. It was the Holy Spirit! How brave they felt now! They ran out into the streets of Jerusalem to tell everyone about Jesus. Three thousand people were baptized with water, and the Church was born.

Today in our church it feels like a party. Everybody wears something red to remind us of the flames of fire. We get red balloons, too. The choir sings music with a beat. We tap our toes because we can feel the Spirit. After each line of our pastor's prayer we say together in a loud voice, "Come, Holy Spirit!" When worship is over, we'll have a cake with real candles to blow out and we'll sing "Happy Birthday, Dear Church." Everyone's invited.

I've heard the Holy Spirit blows where it wants to, like the wind. I've heard the Holy Spirit is closer to us than the air we breathe. I've heard the Holy Spirit is our friend. How can this be?

 God is Spirit.

Trinity

I love to worship God, but sometimes I fidget. Especially during the sermon, because it is long.

Sometimes when I fidget my mom gives me a pencil and paper and says, "Draw what you see." I draw the tall tree just outside the window, or the flowers up front, or the baby peeking over the back of the pew. These remind me of God the Creator. I wonder how God thought up so many different things to create.

Sometimes when I fidget my mom tells me, "Count crosses." I look around and count all the crosses I can find, but my mom always finds one more than I do. All those crosses make me think of God the Son. I wonder why Jesus had to die on the cross.

Sometimes when I fidget my mom bends over and whispers, "Breathe God's air." I take a slow, deep breath in. Then I gently breathe out. In, then out. In, then out. I am breathing God the Spirit!

I wonder how God can be Three in One.

 God is a mystery.

 # All Saints' Day

Do you know any saints? I do. My grandmother and granddad used to read me stories from my children's Bible and teach me prayers. They were saints. Our neighbor goes to the soup kitchen and serves meals to people who don't have food. She is a saint. My best friend is a saint, too, because he plays with a boy during recess that all the other kids pick on. Saints are people who help others know God. We are all saints.

Today we celebrate all the saints we have ever known, and especially the ones who have died. I celebrate my grandmother and granddad. They are with God now. My dad says they are with us, too, but we just can't see them. I wish we could. My dad says they worship God with us. He says they pray with us and sing with us, and they are always here with us during the Lord's Supper.

Today when our pastors serve the bread and the grape juice, I think about Grandmother and Granddad. I wonder where they are sitting. I wonder if they notice how tall I've grown. We sing "For All the Saints," and I cry just a little.

Do you know any saints? You can celebrate them on All Saints' Day.

 There is a little bit of God in everyone.

Advent

It's another new year in our church. Advent. We are waiting for Christmas . . . again. We are waiting and waiting and waiting.

Do you remember lighting the candles on the Advent wreath and counting the Sundays until Christmas? Do you remember the fresh smell of the evergreens that filled the sanctuary? Do you remember how we waited all the way until Christmas Eve for someone to light the Christ candle?

Waiting is hard, but it's not so hard when you wait with me.

Come, worship with me.

 God is very near.

Christian Symbols and Crosses

When you look around inside a church you will probably see some ancient Christian symbols decorating the sanctuary. They might be chiseled from stone, carved in wood, woven or stitched in cloth, or pieced together from bits of colored glass in stained glass windows.

Come With Me *Circle of Eternity*

A circle has no beginning and no ending. Neither does God. God is eternal. God is everywhere. God's love lasts forever.

Psalm 90:1–2

Creator's Star

The Bible says that God created the world in six days. That is why a six-pointed star represents God the Creator. This star also helps us remember six wonderful things about God: power, wisdom, majesty, love, mercy, and justice.

Genesis 1:1–2:3

Advent *Scroll*

The ancient scriptures were written on scrolls. They tell of God's promise to send Israel a savior, and of God's instructions to "prepare ye the way of the Lord." God sent Jesus to be our Lord and Savior. He came to show everyone God's love and power.

Isaiah 40:3, Matthew 1:22–23

Tau Cross

Tau is the last letter of the Hebrew alphabet. The Tau Cross represents all of God's promises in the Hebrew Bible (Old Testament). The Tau Cross is also called the Advent Cross. *Advent* means *coming*. Jesus is coming. God keeps God's promises.

Matthew 1:1, Mark 1:1–3

Christmas *Rose*

The scriptures promised that marvelous things would happen when the Lord came. Sick people would be healed, water would appear in the desert, and roses would bloom there. The rose is a symbol of Jesus. Marvelous things happened when he came to earth.

Isaiah 35:1–2 (KJV)

Anchor Cross

Sailors lower an anchor overboard to steady their ship in a storm. The anchor gives them hope. Jesus is our anchor. He gives hope to the poor, the sick, the prisoners, and anyone who is afraid. He gives hope for peace on earth.

Hebrews 6:19, Luke 2:8–14, 4:18–19

Epiphany *The Five-Pointed Star*

A man named Balaam once said, "a star shall come forth out of Jacob." (Jacob is another name for Israel.) When Jesus was born a very bright star shone in the sky over Bethlehem. Could this be the star that Balaam meant?

Numbers 24:17, Matthew 2:1–12

Cross Crosslet

An *epiphany* is an *appearance* or *showing*. The wise men were the first visitors from the outside world to be shown the baby Jesus. They told others and the good news spread. The arms of this cross end in tiny crosslets, one for each of the four directions on a map.

Luke 13:29

Ordinary Time *Shepherd's Crook*

God wanted the kings of Israel to care for people as a shepherd cares for sheep. Jesus said, "I am the good shepherd." He cares for us more than a regular king could do. Church leaders are sometimes called shepherds. The shepherd's crook symbolizes Christian leadership.

Psalm 23, John 10:11

Latin Cross

Twelve equal squares form the shape of this cross. Twelve friends of Jesus followed him, learned from him, and became the twelve disciples. Now Jesus has millions of disciples. A *disciple* is a *learner* or a *follower*. Are you a disciple?

Luke 5:1–11, Luke 6:12–16

Ash Wednesday *Sacred Monogram: Chi Rho*

In ancient Rome it was against the law to worship Jesus. The early Christians met secretly and left messages for each other in code. They combined the first and second letters of the Greek word for *Christ* (Χριστος) into this secret symbol of Jesus.

Mark 8:27–30

Cross Portate

The Latin word *portate* means *carry*. Jesus was forced to carry his own cross to Golgotha, the place of the skull. When he stumbled, a man named Simon helped him. The Christian life is sometimes called "the way of the cross."

John 19:17, Mark 15:21

The most important symbol for Christians is the cross. Jesus died on a tall cross made of plain, rough wood. Today, crosses of all sizes and patterns are made from materials such as gold, silver, brass, and polished wood. The meaning of each cross and each symbol comes from the Bible and from Christian tradition.

Come To My Church *Hand of God*

God created the world, people, and the Church. We can't see God but sometimes we can feel God. God touches us and helps us to live faithfully. When this happens, we can say that "the hand of God" is upon us.

Genesis 1:1, 31; Hebrews 1:3a

The Ship

The ship is an ancient symbol of the Church. The cross on the sail is an ancient symbol of Jesus. A sail gives a ship power to move through the waters. Jesus gives the Church power to love God and serve others. He offers that same power to everyone.

1 John 5:1–5

Crown

Israel's greatest king was David. Jesus was David's great, great grandson. God made Jesus the "King of Kings."

Matthew 1:1–16, Revelation 19:16

Blue or Purple Candles

We call Jesus *Emmanuel*, which means *God-with-Us*. Four candles help us count down the Sundays until his birthday. The candles are blue (color of royalty) or purple (color of waiting). The third one can be pink. It is the candle of joy.

Isaiah 7:14, Luke 1:26–33

Christ Candle

When the people Israel were prisoners in Babylon, Isaiah comforted them with a promise from God. "The people who walked in darkness have seen a great light," said Isaiah. This promise came true when Jesus was born. Jesus is "the light of the world."

Isaiah 9:2, 6; John 8:12

Lion

God formed Israel from twelve different tribes of people. One of those tribes was named Judah. Judah was so powerful that it was compared to a lion. Jesus is a descendant of that tribe. He is called the "lion of Judah."

Genesis 49:8–10, Revelation 5:5

Shell

Another *epiphany* happened when Jesus was baptized. God showed Jesus to hundreds of people and said, "This is my beloved Son." Today, some pastors baptize people using a shell to scoop and pour the water. Shells remind us of Jesus' baptism, and of Epiphany.

Luke 3:21–22

Jerusalem Cross

The four small crosses in between the central arms of this cross represent north, south, east, and west. The Church began in Jerusalem. Then people like Peter and Paul started new churches in other cities. Now there are churches nearly everywhere in the world.

Matthew 28:16–20, Luke 24:44–48

Shields of the Apostles

The twelve disciples were also called *apostles*, which means *sent out*. Jesus sent his friends out to preach the *gospel*, which means the *good news*. The apostles were the first leaders of the Church. It was not easy for them. People made fun of them, threw stones at them, and even put them in prison, but the apostles trusted the Holy Spirit to shield them. Christian symbols in the shape of shields stand for each of the apostles. The designs on the shields tell us about their lives.

Matthew 10:1–4

Rainbow

Once, when evil filled the earth, God sent a great flood. Only Noah and his family were saved. Afterward God promised never to do that again, and God put a rainbow in the sky. When we do wrong things, God will not destroy us. God will forgive us.

Genesis 9:8–17, 1 John 1:8–9

Dove

After the great flood, Noah sent out a dove from the ark. When the dove came back carrying an olive branch, Noah knew that all was well again. The dove represents peace between God and the world. It also represents peace among people.

Genesis 8:6–12

Lent

Praying Hands

Jesus prayed alone and with others. The night before he died, he prayed in a garden for many hours. He taught his friends a perfect prayer, called the "Lord's Prayer," or the "Our Father." Do you know the words?

Matthew 6:9–13, 26:36–46

Cross of Four Phaeons

The arms of this cross end in tiny *phaeons*, or darts. When we are tempted to do wrong things, it can seem like someone is shooting darts at us to wear us down. When we pray, God helps us to be faithful.

Ephesians 6:1

Palm Sunday   *Crown with a Cross*

On Palm Sunday people wanted to crown Jesus as their king, but on Good Friday they watched him die on the cross. "Be faithful unto death," the Bible says, "and I will give you the crown of life."

Revelation 2:10

Passion Cross

The sharp tips of this cross cause us to think about the *passion,* or *suffering,* of Christ. Another name for "Palm Sunday" is "Passion Sunday," because it is the first day of Holy Week, the week in which Jesus suffered and died.

Luke 18:31–34, 19:28–4

Maundy Thursday   *The Pelican*

Long ago, people believed a mother pelican would pierce her chest with her beak to feed her babies with her own blood. When Jesus served wine to his friends at the Last Supper, he said, "This is my blood." The pelican is a symbol of Jesus.

Matthew 26:26–29

The Cross with Crown of Thorns

The soldiers who arrested Jesus twisted branches of a thorn bush into the shape of a crown. Laughing, they put it on Jesus' head. Then they whipped Jesus and led him out to be killed.

Matthew 27:11–14, 24–31

Good Friday   *Inscription on the Cross*

Jesus was innocent, but the authorities posted a sign on his cross accusing him of trying to become king. The sign said, "Jesus of Nazareth, King of the Jews" (in Latin, *"Iesus Nazarenus Rex Iudaeorum"*). The first letter of each Latin word forms the symbol *INRI*.

John 19:19–21

Crucifix

When we close our hearts to God and do wrong things, we sin. God feels sad and we feel guilty. Jesus saved us from our guilt and sin by dying on the cross. Jesus is called the *Christ,* which means *Messiah* or *Savior.*

John 3:16–17, 1 Corinthians 15:3–5

Easter   *Agnus Dei (Lamb of God)*

When the Israelites were slaves in Egypt, they put lamb's blood on their doorposts and God saved them from a deadly plague. Jesus is the *Lamb of God.* By bleeding, dying, and rising again, he saved us from our sins. His banner is a symbol of triumph.

Exodus 12:1–13, John 1:29

Cross in Glory

On Easter we celebrate how splendid and magnificent God is to raise Jesus from death. The glorious rays streaming outward from this cross form the shape of a sunburst, showing that "the light of the world" has returned.

John 8:12, Luke 24:1–12

Pentecost   *Seven-Tongued Flame*

Seven tongues of fire stand for the "seven gifts of the Spirit" (Isaiah 11:2–3). See Galatians 5:22 for more gifts ("fruits") of the Spirit. The disciples received the gift of courage on Pentecost. What gifts has the Spirit given you?

Isaiah 11:2–3, Galatians 5:22–23

Cross Flambant

Flambant means *flaming* in French. The tiny flames of fire lining the edges of this cross resemble the flames seen by Jesus' friends on Pentecost. The Holy Spirit helps us to be "on fire" for God!

Acts 2:1–13

Trinity   *Triquetra*

The three equal parts of the triquetra connected together depict the Triune God. *Triune* means *three-in-one.* God is the Creator (Father), God is the Son (Jesus), and God is the Holy Spirit (Holy Ghost).

Matthew 28:16–20

Latin Cross Bottonnée (Budded Cross)

Three flower petals decorate the ends of the arms of this cross. They represent the Father, the Son, and the Holy Spirit, who are not three gods, but "one God in three persons." This is the meaning of the word *Trinity.*

2 Corinthians 1:20–22

All Saints' Day   *Alpha and Omega*

The Greek alphabet begins with Alpha (A) and ends with Omega (Ω). Our lives begin and end with God. We can say that God is with us from A to Z.

Revelation 21:6

Celtic Cross

The unending circle in the center of this Irish cross represents the never-ending love of Christ. When we follow him we become part of the *communion of saints.* The Bible says, "Nothing can separate us from the love of God in Christ."

Romans 8:38–39, 1 Corinthians 1:2

Golden Calf

The Israelites lived in the desert for a long time: forty years. They complained a lot. Once, they turned away from God and worshiped a golden calf. During Lent we try not to turn away from God. Lent lasts a long time: forty days and six Sundays.

Exodus 32:1–35

Rooster

The disciple Peter promised to stand by Jesus until the very end. Jesus answered, "Before the rooster crows twice, you will deny me three times." After Jesus was arrested, Peter did just that. Then a rooster crowed, and Peter wept.

Mark 14:26–31, 66–72

Palm Branches

In ancient times, palm branches were a sign of victory. Early Christians carved palms onto the walls of their hiding places to celebrate Jesus' victory over death. These carvings can still be seen today.

John 11:12–13, 43–44; Revelation 7:9

Three Nails

When Jesus was crucified, his hands and feet were nailed to the cross. When Jesus rose again, he showed his friends the marks of the nails and they knew it was really him.

John 20:19–29

Thistle

The symbol of the thistle is used during Lent to represent the sorrow and suffering of Jesus. The spines on its stalk are sharp like the thorns of the crown that Jesus wore.

Luke 24:45–47

Spider

When Jesus sat down for the Last Supper, he already knew one of his friends would betray him. Just as a spider spins a web and waits for its prey, so the enemies of Jesus waited to capture him.

Matthew 26:20–25

Jeweled Cross

Jesus was the Son of God, but he was a real person, too. When he was crucified he bled from his hands, his feet, and a wound in his side. The jewels in this cross stand for the five wounds of Jesus. They are red, the color of blood.

John 19:31–37

Owl

A psalm in the Bible says, "I am like an owl of the desert." That is how lonely Jesus felt when he died. Most of his friends had deserted him. Had God deserted him, too?

Mark 15:33–39, Psalm 102:6

Butterfly

The caterpillar inside its cocoon reminds Christians of Jesus sealed in his tomb. The butterfly emerging from the cocoon reminds Christians of Jesus rising again from death and surprising all his friends.

Matthew 28:1–10

Frog

During dry months, many frogs hide under leaves or in soil to stay moist. When the rains return, the frogs reappear just as suddenly as Jesus reappeared from death. Have you ever heard the "peepers" in early spring? These frogs sing like choirs of tiny angels.

Psalm 100, Psalm 148

Descending Dove

A dove facing downward symbolizes the Holy Spirit. When Jesus was baptized, the Spirit came down from the sky in the shape of a dove. The Spirit comes down to us, too, when we are baptized. Have you been baptized?

Mark 1:9–11

Fish

In Greek, the first letters of the words, "Jesus Christ, Son of God, Savior," spell "ΙΧΘΥΣ" (icthus), or "fish." Jesus said, "Follow me, and I will make you fish for people." The fish was an early, secret symbol of the Church and of the Lord's Supper.

Mark 1:16–18

Triangle

We can pray to the Father, or to the Son, or to the Holy Spirit, or to all three. The Father, Son, and Holy Spirit are equal to each other in every way. That is why a triangle with three equal sides represents the *Trinity*.

2 Corinthians 13:13

Interwoven Circles

God was here before time began and God will still be here after time ends. Three overlapping circles show that God—Father, Son, and Holy Spirit—is eternal. God was and is and ever shall be.

Revelation 4:8

Peacock

When a peacock sheds its beautiful tail feathers, another set just as magnificent grows back. In medieval times, people thought that dead peacocks would never decay. For these reasons the peacock symbolizes *immortality* (never-ending life with God).

1 Corinthians 15:53–55

Phoenix

Legend tells of a mythical bird that lived for 500 years, then built a nest and burned itself up. Three days later it rose again from its ashes. For Christians, the phoenix became a symbol of *resurrection*. Jesus' resurrection opened the way to eternal life for all.

John 11:25–26